D1411495

THE *Little Book* OF

~

THOUGHTFUL
MOMENTS

~

A BEAUTIFUL COLLECTION
OF GENTLE WORDS AND
FINE ART

Editor: Fleur Robertson
Editorial Assistance: Kirsty Wheeler
Original Design Concept: Peter Bridgewater
Design: Stonecastle Graphics Ltd
Design Assistance: Sally Strugnell
Director of Production: Gerald Hughes
Production: Ruth Arthur, Sally Connolly, Neil Randles
Typesetting: Julie Smith

Published by
CHARTWELL BOOKS, INC.
A Division of Book Sales, Inc.
POST OFFICE BOX 7100
114 Northfield Avenue
Edison, NJ 08818-7100

CLB 3144
© 1993 Colour Library Books Ltd
Godalming, Surrey, England.
Printed and bound in Singapore.
All rights reserved.
ISBN 1 55521 992 6

THE *Little Book* OF
THOUGHTFUL
MOMENTS

CHARTWELL
BOOKS, INC.

Introduction

*I*t is surely wise once in a while to pause and take stock of life, to reflect and ponder on the direction we are taking, the routes we have traveled, the decisions we have made and will make. Such times – those quiet moments that arrive when we are alone – are times to consider the views and visions that feature in the following pages. The words and the work of some of the world's greatest writers and artists can inspire us then, and their understanding shed light on our lives. Just a line, a few sentences may start a train of thought that brings the mind to a happy conclusion, the heart to rest.

As the poet said, "Great thoughts come from the heart." Here is such a selection.

Within Us

The days that make us
happy make us wise.

John Masefield

What lies behind us, and what lies
before us are tiny matters,
compared to what lies within us.

Ralph Waldo Emerson

Memories

Let Fate do her worst, there are relics of joy,
Bright dreams of the past, which she cannot destroy!
Which come in the night-time of sorrow and care,
And bring back the features that joy used to wear.
Long, long be my heart with such memories filled!
Like the vase in which roses have once been distilled;
You may break, you may ruin the vase if you will,
But the scent of the roses will hang round it still.

Thomas Moore

Friendship

....

There's nothing worth the wear of
winning, but laughter and
the love of friends.

Hilaire Belloc

Friendship is unnecessary, like
philosophy, like art .... It has no
survival value; rather it is one of those
things that give value to survival.

C.S. Lewis

14

Life May Perfect Be

It is not growing like a tree
In bulk, doth make man better be;
Or standing long an oak, three hundred year,
To fall a log at last, dry, bald, and sear:
A lily of the day
Is fairer far in May,
Although it fall and die that night, –
It was the plant and flower of Light.
In small proportions we just beauties see;
And in short measure life may perfect be.

Ben Jonson

Friends Together

We have been friends together,
In sunshine and in shade;
Since first beneath the chestnut trees
In infancy we played.
But coldness dwells within thy heart –
A cloud is on thy brow;
We have been friends together –
Shall a light word part us now?

Caroline Norton

Friends

*Y*ou can make more friends in two
months by becoming interested in
other people than you can in two
years of trying to get other
people interested in you.

Dale Carnegie

*N*o love, no friendship can cross the
path of our destiny without leaving
some mark on it forever.

Francois Mauriac

Experience

*Experience is a hard teacher
because she gives the test first,
the lesson afterwards.*

Vernon Law

*Sometimes the readiness to be sorry
can appear in a flash of insight; other
times it may cost a sleepless night
or a long sulk. Either way, you've got
to go through the process.*

Lawrence Shames

Sunshine

Those who bring sunshine to the
lives of others cannot keep it
from themselves.

J. M. Barrie

Is it so small a thing
To have enjoy'd the sun
To have lived light in the spring
To have loved, to have thought,
to have done?

Matthew Arnold

Love and Time

Love and Time with reverence use,
Treat them like a parting friend;
Nor the golden gifts refuse
Which in youth sincere they send:
For each year their price is more,
And less simple than before.

John Dryden

Old Friends

*M*ake new friends, but keep the old;
Those are silver, these are gold.
New-made friendships, like new wine,
Age will mellow and refine.
Friendships that have stood the test –
Time and change – are surely best;
Brow may wrinkle, hair grow gray;
Friendship never knows decay.
For 'mid old friends, tried and true,
Once more we our youth renew.

Joseph Parry

A Garden's Pleasure

God Almighty first planted a garden.
And indeed it is the purest of human
pleasures ... the greatest refreshment
to the spirits of man.

Francis Bacon

In your garden you can walk
And with each plant and flower talk
View all their glories, from each one
Raise some rare meditation.

John Rea

Today's Roses

One of the most tragic things I know about human nature is that all of us tend to put off living. We are all dreaming about some magical rose garden over the horizon – instead of enjoying the roses that are blooming outside our windows today.

Dale Carnegie

Love Alone

Love alone is capable of uniting
living beings in such a way as to complete
and fulfill them, for it alone takes them
and joins them by what is deepest
in themselves.

Pierre Teilhard de Chardin

That best portion of a good man's life,
His little, nameless, unremembered acts
Of kindess and of love.

William Wordsworth

A Happy Life

All shall be well
and all shall be well
and all manner of things
shall be well.

Julian of Norwich

A happy life must be to a great
extent a quiet life, for it is only in an
atmosphere of quiet that
true joy can live.

Bertrand Russell

Morning

The year's at the spring
And day's at the morn;
Morning's at seven;
The hillside's dew-pearled;
The lark's on the wing;
The snail's on the thorn:
God's in his heaven —
All's right with the world.

Robert Browning

39

Love's Beginning

The power of a glance has been so much abused in love stories that it has come to be disbelieved in. Few people dare now to say that two beings have fallen in love because they have looked at each other. Yet it is in this way that love begins, and in this way only. The rest is only the rest and comes afterwards. Nothing is more real than these great shocks which two souls give each other in exchanging this spark.

Victor Hugo

A Good Friend

$\mathcal{I}$ want a warm and faithful friend,
To cheer the adverse hour;
Who ne'er to flatter will descend,
Nor bend the knee to power, –
A friend to chide me when I'm wrong,
My inmost soul to see;
And that my friendship prove as strong
For him as his for me.

John Quincy Adams

An Identity of Souls

Friendship and loyalty are in an
identity of souls seldom found on
earth. The only really lasting and
valuable friendship is between
people of a similar nature.

Mahatma Gandhi

Tell me who admires and loves you,
and I will tell you who you are.

Charles Augustin Sainte-Beuve

One Happy Hour

The garland I send thee was culled from those bowers
Where thou and I wandered in long vanished hours;
Not a leaf or a blossom its bloom here displays,
But bears some remembrance of those happy days.

The roses were gathered by that garden gate,
Where our meetings, though early, seemed always late;
Where ling'ring full oft through a summer-night's moon,
Our partings, though late, appeared always too soon.

The rest were all culled from the banks of that glade,
Where, watching the sunset, so often we stayed,
And mourned, as the time went, that Love had no power
To bind in his chain even one happy hour.

Thomas Moore

Happiness

··

*O*ne is happy as a result of one's
own efforts, once one knows the
necessary ingredients of happiness –
simple tastes, a certain degree of
courage, self-denial to a point, love of
work, and, above all, a clear
conscience. Happiness is no vague
dream, of that I now feel certain.

Georges Sand

The Whole Heart

*O*h, the miraculous energy that flows
between two people who care enough
to get beyond surfaces and games, who
are willing to take the risks of being
totally open, of listening, of responding
with the whole heart. How much we
can do for each other!

Alex Noble

*O*f all the gifts that wise Providence
grants us to make life full and happy,
friendship is the most beautiful.

Epicurus

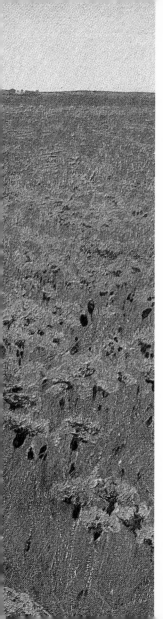

The Better Land

In all places, then, and in all seasons,
Flowers expand their light and soul-like wings,
Teaching us, by most persuasive reasons,
How akin they are to human things.

And with childlike, credulous affection,
We behold their tender buds expand –
Emblems of our own great resurrection,
Emblems of the bright and better land.

Henry Wadsworth Longfellow

Mothers and Children

*Y*outh fades; love droops, the leaves
of friendship fall: a mother's secret
hope outlives them all.

Oliver Wendall Holmes

*C*hildren have neither past nor
future; they enjoy the present,
which very few of us do.

Jean de la Bruyère

To Have Succeeded

To laugh often and love much, to win
the respect of intelligent persons and the
affection of children; to earn the
approbation of honest critics and to endure
the betrayal of false friends; to appreciate
beauty; to find the best in others; to give
one's self; to leave the world a bit better,
whether by a healthy child, a garden patch
or a redeemed social condition; to have
played and laughed with enthusiasm and
sung with exultation; to know even one life
has breathed easier because you have lived,
this is to have succeeded.

Ralph Waldo Emerson

Courage

I am only one, but still I am one.
I cannot do everything, but still
I can do something. I will not refuse
to do the something I can do.

Helen Keller

*L*ife is mostly froth and bubble,
Two things stand like stone,
Kindness in another's trouble,
Courage in your own.

Adam Lindsey Gordon

Acknowledgements

The publishers would like to thank the following for permission to reproduce. ART RESOURCE, New York, with acknowledgements to Giraudon, Paris, for *Resting at a Brook*/Sisley, pp. 10-11; *Landscape at Eragny*/Pissarro, pp. 24-25; *Woman in a Garden*/Graves, p. 31. A.K.G., Berlin, for *Girls in a Field of Cornflowers*/Ring, pp. 52-53 and with acknowledgements to: Leipzig Museum of Fine Arts for *Girl in a Poppyfield*/Hitz, p. 16; Skahens Museum for *Summer Evening on Skagen Beach*/Kroeger, pp. 28-29; Tournai Museum of Fine Arts for *Argenteuil*/Manet, p. 35; Washington National Gallery for *The Boating Party*/Cassatt, pp. 42-43; Boston Museum of Fine Arts for *Camille Monet and Child*/Monet, pp. 54-55. THE BRIDGEMAN ART LIBRARY, London, with acknowledgements to Christies, London, for *Girl in a red dress reading by a swimming pool*/Lavery, p. 8; Warrington Museum and Art Gallery, Lancs., for *Rosina*/Woods, p. 12; City of Bristol Museum and Art Gallery for *Holidays*/Watson, pp. 14-15; Roy Miles Fine Art Paintings, London, for *The Orchard*/Erichson, p. 19; the Curtis Brown Group Ltd, London, (copyright Dame Laura Knight) for *In the Field*/Knight, pp. 20-21; Musée du Petit Palais, Paris, and Giraudon, Paris, for *Portrait of a Young Woman*/Aman-Jean, p. 23; a private collection for *Nerissa*/Godward, p. 27; the Fine Art Society, London, for Roses/Kroyer, p. 32; Connaught Brown, London, for *Girl Reading in a Sunlit Room*/Holsoe, pp. 26-27; Bradford Art Galleries and Museums for *The Garden*/Walker, p. 46, and for *The Orchard*/La Thangue, p. 50; Christopher Wood Gallery, London, for *Portrait of Lady Sutherland*/Ward, p. 59. CHRISTIES IMAGES, London, for *Lady in an Interior*/Holsoe, jacket. FINE ART PHOTOGRAPHIC LIBRARY, London, for *Picking Posies by the River Bourne*/Mackay, facing and title page, and with acknowledgements to Galerie Berko for *In the Poppy Field*/Giran-Max, pp. 38-39; a private collection for *Love at first sight*/Volkhart, pp. 40-41; N. R. Orrell Gallery, London, for *Grandfather's Pet*/Snape, pp. 44-45; City Wall Gallery for *At Hampton Lucy, Warwickshire*/Mackay, pp. 48-49; Anthony Mitchell Paintings, Nottingham, for *Summer's Delight*/Seeger, p.57.